WORKBOOK

FIGHTING YOUR BATTLES

JONATHAN EVANS

H®

HARVEST HOUSE PUBLISHERS
EUGENE, OREGON

Cover design by Faceout Studios, Spencer Fuller

Cover photo © subbery / Shutterstock

Interior design by KUHN Design Group

For bulk, special sales, or ministry purchases, please call 1-800-547-8979. Email: Customerservice@hhpbooks.com

Fighting Your Battles Workbook
Copyright © 2022 by Jonathan Evans
Published by Harvest House Publishers
Eugene, Oregon 97408
www.harvesthousepublishers.com

ISBN 978-0-7369-8434-8 (pbk.)
ISBN 978-0-7369-8435-5 (eBook)

CONTENTS

ACKNOWLEDGMENTS

I'd like to thank my friends at Harvest House Publishers, particularly Bob Hawkins and Steve Miller, for their vision and support for this message I'm so passionate about. And thank you to Kim Moore, for coordinating everyone's efforts and seeing this project through to the finish.

I'm also grateful for Phil Warner, Will Irwin, and the rest of the team at RightNow Media for their excellence and expertise in producing the video that accompanies this workbook, as well as for steering the overall direction of the workbook itself—always with an eternal perspective in mind. I'm happy to team up with you guys anytime!

Finally, thank you to Kris Bearss, who collaborated so skillfully with me to adapt my content and ideas so that individuals and groups can study the Word, not just hear it and read it.

I pray that, through the collective use of our gifts, God will get the glory, turning these materials into tools that help every believer faithfully entrust their battles to the Lord so that they may stand firm and experience the victory He has already won.

MAKING THE MOST OF THIS WORKBOOK/ PARTICIPANT'S GUIDE

This workbook and guide is a tool to help your group combine the video and subsequent Bible study into a dynamic growth experience. If you are the leader or facilitator of your group, take some time in advance to consider the questions in the Video Group Discussion and Group Bible Exploration sections of this guide, and then come up with personal examples to encourage discussion. Also make sure each individual has their own workbook, which will allow them to take notes during the group time as well as dig deeper on their own throughout the week.

Because every group session includes a video portion, think about the logistics. Before the session, ensure that everyone will be able to see the screen clearly and that the audio is set at a comfortable level. You don't want your group to miss anything.

Now let's preview the sections in each of the six sessions.

VIDEO TEACHING NOTES

Several key points and quotes from the video are provided in this section, along with room to write notes.

VIDEO GROUP DISCUSSION

Many of the discussion questions have to do with remembering what was just viewed, and this immediate follow-up is important—we can forget content unless we review it right away. Other questions in this section try to connect the video to emotions or experience: *How did you feel when Jonathan said that? Is that true in your life? Do you have the same issue?*

GROUP BIBLE EXPLORATION

This is a Bible study, so each session is grounded in Scripture. And because different levels of faith may be found within your group, this time in the Bible is to not only grow but to help others find their faith.

IN CLOSING

The goal for every Bible study is to apply what's learned. This section highlights the main point of the session and challenges participants to dive deeper.

ON YOUR OWN BETWEEN SESSIONS

This section includes additional study that participants can do to keep the content they just learned fresh in their minds throughout the week, and it challenges participants to dive deeper.

RECOMMENDED READING

Your group time will be enhanced if everyone reads the recommended chapters in *Fighting Your Battles* by Jonathan Evans before the next session. Jonathan's video teaching follows the book, but the book has considerably more information and illustrations. Everyone is encouraged to prepare ahead by reading the designated chapters.

UNDERSTANDING THE BATTLE

Every life has its battles. Jesus was up-front about that. He warned His followers, "Hey, don't be surprised. In this world, you're going to endure many troubles." But He also assured the faithful again and again that these trials and tribulations aren't a sign that God has abandoned them. Just the opposite. Throughout the Bible we see that the Lord has equipped and called each of us to fight—and win—those battles for our good and His glory.

Thankfully, He doesn't expect any of us to achieve the victory ourselves. This entire study is geared toward the truth that *every battle of yours is His, and He has already overcome whatever (or whoever) is coming against you.* So there's no need for worry or dread. God has the battle plan for each setting you'll be sent into, He's prepared the Playbook for each type of opponent you'll face, and He is equipping you to conquer any obstacles that will ever stand in your way.

Over six sessions, author and speaker Jonathan Evans will revisit some of the Bible's "battle-grounds" and "foxholes"—the situations and places where the faith of God's people was severely tested. As he digs deep into the internal battles those believers fought, he'll help each of us understand and prepare to conquer the challenges and challengers that *will* come our way. This is important because, in the middle of a storm…a wilderness…a pit…a bitter conflict, even seasoned warriors sometimes lose sight of the reality that really changes the game: the reality that if the Lord is with you, nothing and no one can defeat you. This study will help to train your soul in that truth, so that you'll carry it with you like a banner and a shield wherever the Lord calls you.

Before you watch Jonathan's first video, here's an excerpt from the opening chapter of his book *Fighting Your Battles*. It centers on David's tremendous declaration in 1 Samuel 17, just before he took on Goliath—and won:

"The battle is the LORD's." Those were David's words (verse 47), but they have to be our battle cry too. Every battle we will ever face belongs to God.

In those times when the battle really beats you up and you get overwhelmed, it's usually for one of two reasons: either you're running into the fight on your own power or you've tried to own what isn't yours.

Running toward the giant without God's power is going to get you crushed. By yourself, you simply don't possess what's necessary in order to overcome. I don't; David didn't; my family didn't [when my mom was diagnosed with cancer]. With God, however, every one of us possesses what's necessary. We must enter the battle in His power.

The second reason we can end up overwhelmed is because we've taken the ownership role instead of the stewardship role. You and I are supposed to be stewards of the battle, not owners of the battle. So recognize who really owns it. This is one of those statements that takes the monkey off people's backs. The One who owns it is Lord over it. The Owner has the power. He can defeat anyone or anything that comes against Him or His people.

No matter what others think, the battle is the Lord's. No matter what the giant says about you, no matter how your family or your boss might doubt you, you cannot lose if the fight is His. You might look like a flea compared to the giant you're up against, but looks don't win.

The God of heaven and earth is with you. The Warrior of all the ages fights for you. The battle is the Lord's.

Your victory is sure.

Fighting Your Battles, pages 28-29

VIDEO TEACHING NOTES

As you watch the video, use the space on the next page to take notes. Some key points and quotables are provided as reminders.

Main Idea

- God chooses the faithful to face giants and to fight battles for our strengthening and for His kingdom. These difficult times are a part of every Christian's calling.

- Because of Christ's victory on the cross, anyone who puts their trust in Him is "more than a conqueror" before they ever step foot in the ring. God places you in situations where you can use your passion, your opportunities, your abilities, and your experiences to defeat any giant.

- Knowing that the win has already been won should give you a different view of both the battle and your giant. Others may be paralyzed by fear, or by the size of the problem, but those who are called see the size of the God who calls them instead.

- As you become surer of who you are in Christ, you'll recognize the ways God has equipped and prepared you to defeat the giant who is standing before you. Then, like David, you can run to the battle with full confidence that the Lord will fight for you.

- We overcome, not by our might, but God's.

- Personal Notes:

Application

If God has called you, then God is for you. And if God is for you, then you can be confident that no giant can stand against you.

Quotables

- A lot of Christians today are fighting for victory instead of fighting from victory. They don't understand the fact that we've already been called for this battle. We've already been called to overcome. We already have the call of "conqueror."

- All the things that you've overcome in your life are just to prepare you for this next moment, and to let you know that your calling is much bigger than your giant.

- The battle is necessary for the victory to be experienced.

VIDEO GROUP DISCUSSION

1. On each continuum below, mark an *X* where you would place yourself in response to the question.

   How do you tend to view the giants in your life?

   Opposition   Opportunity

   _____

How do you tend to view yourself when a giant shows up wanting to fight?

Victim   Victor

_____

How do you tend to view your position when the giant shows up wanting to fight?

Called Out and Exposed   Called and Covered

_____

How do you tend to view the words of the Lord as you prepare for battle?

Highly Questionable   Fully Reliable

_____

How do you tend to view God in your battles?

Absent   Present

_____

2. Besides the size of our opponents, what are some of the other characteristics of our giants that sidetrack us?

   What concerns or barriers have you seen Satan use to keep people from recognizing who they are in the Lord? In what ways does the evil one blind us, limit us, or limit God's power in our minds and hearts?

3. For David, knowing that he'd been called to the battle *and* called to conquer affected everything as he was "entering the ring" to fight Goliath, including his preparation. Think of a particular opponent you've faced in the past. How would your preparation and approach have changed if you had trusted that the Lord had called you, equipped you, and would fight for you in that situation?

What difference does it make to know that the opponents and difficulties that come at us are never just random circumstance, and are often part of our calling from God?

4. One of the verses that serves as a foundation for Jonathan's teaching in this session is Romans 8:37. What do you think is meant by the assurance that we "overwhelmingly conquer through Him who loved us"? Why would the Lord describe our victory in these words?

5. Have someone read Romans 8:29-30 out loud, which is another key passage for this session. God has very intentionally "drafted" each person for His championship team. What does that say about how He views and values us?

GROUP BIBLE EXPLORATION

1. The people of Israel faced a different type of giant earlier in the Bible, as they were anticipating the Promised Land. Read and discuss these passages from the book of Numbers, when Moses sent twelve spies on a reconnaissance mission into enemy territory while the Israelites were in the wilderness. Then answer each question.

   > The LORD spoke to Moses, saying, "Send out men for yourself to spy out the land of Canaan, which I am going to give the sons of Israel; you shall send a man from each of their fathers' tribes, every one a leader among them." (13:1-2)

   The Lord's instruction includes two important details—one about the land of Canaan and one about the men being chosen for the assignment. How should these two realities have set the tone for the entire group's mission?

2. Notice the differences in the reports of the spies after they returned from spying out the land:

- They brought back word to [Moses and Aaron] and to all the congregation…"We came into the land where you sent us, and it certainly does flow with milk and honey, and this is its fruit. Nevertheless, the people who live in the land are strong, and the cities are fortified and very large." (13:26-28)

- Then Caleb quieted the people before Moses and said, "We should by all means go up and take possession of it, for we will certainly prevail over it." But the men who had gone up with him said, "We are not able to go up against the people, because they are too strong for us…The land through which we have gone to spy out is a land that devours its inhabitants; and all the people whom we saw in it are people of great stature…We were like grasshoppers in our own sight, and so we were in their sight." (13:30-33)

- Then all the congregation raised their voices and cried out, and the people wept that night. And all the sons of Israel grumbled against Moses and Aaron…[Joshua and Caleb] tore their clothes; and they spoke to all the congregation…, saying, "The land which we passed through to spy out is an exceedingly good land. If the LORD is pleased with us, then He will bring us into this land and give it to us—a land which flows with milk and honey. Only do not rebel against the LORD; and do not fear the people of the land, for they will be our prey. Their protection is gone from them, and the LORD is with us; do not fear them." (14:1-2, 6-9)

How would you characterize the focus of each "faction": the ten spies, Joshua and Caleb, and the congregation or community of Israelites?

The ten spies—

Joshua and Caleb—

The congregation—

What specific truths were Caleb and Joshua relying on? Where did their confidence come from?

Why do you think the people almost unanimously believed the bad report of the ten spies instead of Caleb and Joshua's good report, which aligned with the word of the Lord about Israel's future?

Why are longtime believers—and even Christian leaders—sometimes prone to doubt and panic despite God's promises-in-advance that we will win?

3. In Numbers 14, Caleb and Joshua are held up as godly examples who were rewarded for their faith (verses 30, 38). Specifically, the Lord said of Caleb: "Because he has had a different spirit and has followed Me fully, I will bring him into the land which he entered, and his descendants shall take possession of it" (verse 24).

   What two qualities distinguished Caleb from the ten spies?

4. Many of the wins we read about in Scripture weren't just for the men and women of Bible times. In powerful verses like the ones below, God has promised His people victory today against their giants too. Read each one of these aloud:

   • "No weapon that is formed against you will succeed; and you will condemn every tongue that accuses you in judgment. This is the heritage of the servants of the LORD, and their vindication is from Me," declares the LORD. (Isaiah 54:17)

   • Greater is He who is in you than he who is in the world. (1 John 4:4)

   • You are a chosen people, a royal priesthood, a holy nation, a people for God's own possession, so that you may proclaim the excellencies of Him who has called you out of darkness into His marvelous light. (1 Peter 2:9)

- Whoever has been born of God overcomes the world; and this is the victory that has overcome the world: our faith. (1 John 5:4)

How can believers reset their focus and develop "a different spirit" so that the giants in life don't intimidate them?

IN CLOSING

As you end the study today, share prayer requests related to the giants you're each facing. Be honest about where you feel you need a more God-focused perspective or assurance of your calling. Ask the Holy Spirit to open up your heart throughout this study so you can receive the truths of Scripture and victoriously live out your faith. And rebuke the discouragement and fear that the enemy wants to put in your path.

Before Session 2, complete the "On Your Own Between Sessions" section below.

ON YOUR OWN BETWEEN SESSIONS

1. Have you ever believed you would win while a "giant" of an opponent was standing right in front of you? What was the source of your confidence? Ego? Faith? The "odds" being in your favor? Your own strength?

   What was the outcome? What did you learn from that experience that better equipped you for the future?

2. Read each Bible passage below and answer:

- What was the believer's perspective?

- How did they view their position?

- What action(s) did they take as a result?

"After we had already suffered and been treated abusively in Philippi, as you know, we had the boldness in our God to speak to you the gospel of God amid much opposition…Just as we have been approved by God to be entrusted with the gospel, so we speak, not intending to please people, but to please God, who examines our hearts." (1 Thessalonians 2:2-4)

Perspective:

Position:

Action:

"Fierce men stir up strife against me…Each evening they come back, howling like dogs and prowling about the city. There they are, bellowing with their mouths with swords in their lips—for 'Who,' they think, 'will hear us?' But you, O Lord, laugh at them; you hold all the nations in derision. O my Strength, I will watch for you, for you, O God, are my fortress. My God in his steadfast love will meet me; God will let me look in triumph on my enemies." (Psalm 59:3, 6-10 ESV)

Perspective:

Position:

Action:

"The next day the rulers, the elders and the teachers of the law met in Jerusalem…They had Peter and John brought before them and began to question them: 'By what power or what name did you do this?' Then Peter, filled with the Holy Spirit, said to them: 'Rulers and elders of the people! If we are being called to account today for an act of kindness shown to a man who was lame and are being asked how he was healed, then know this, you and all the people of Israel: It is by the name of Jesus Christ of Nazareth, whom you crucified but whom God raised from the dead, that this man stands before you healed…Salvation is found in no one else, for there is no other name under heaven given to mankind by which we must be saved.' When they saw the courage of Peter and John and realized that they were unschooled, ordinary men, they were astonished and they took note that these men had been with Jesus." (Acts 4:5, 7-10, 12-13)

Perspective:

Position:

Action:

3. What's typically your goal in times of battle? To just survive? To feel as little pain as possible? To see what you're made of? To become stronger?

What might be God's goal by sometimes placing you in tough situations that are too big for you to handle alone?

4. How does it make you feel that the Lord is not only willing but actually *will* fight for you? What does it mean to you to have someone defend you and enter the ring with you?

5. Which people or circumstances in your life have actually or almost affected your battle perspective in a negative way? For example, who added excess weight, wanting you to wear their armor? Or what situation promoted a fear that you've carried with you?

What do you need to discard so that you can run to the battle exactly how God has equipped and prepared you?

6. David drew on his previous defeats of the lion and the bear as he considered how God would help him against Goliath. Why is remembrance of past victories with the Lord such an important part of a Christian's spiritual arsenal?

On page 26 of the book, Jonathan writes: "[David] ran toward the battle because, even though this challenger was bigger than the lion and the bear, David's God was the Almighty, the Lord of heaven and earth, the faithful Deliverer who never fails. The Lord would do again what the Lord has always done."

What are some of the things the Lord has always done for you, even before you gave your life to Him?

How has He prepared you through your past for the giant you're facing now?

Take courage in this! It's just one more proof that God will go with you!

7. Put your faith into practice. Whatever giant you're facing, pray Psalm 35:1-3 each day of this week as a reminder that your battle is the Lord's.

> Contend, LORD, with those who contend with me;
> Fight against those who fight against me.
> Take hold of buckler and shield
> And rise up as my help.
> Draw also the spear and the battle-axe to meet those who pursue me;
> Say to my soul, "I am your salvation."

RECOMMENDED READING

In preparation for Session 2, please read chapters 2–3 in *Fighting Your Battles* by Jonathan Evans.

THE GOD ABOVE THE BATTLE

Here's an excerpt from *Fighting Your Battles*, when the Israelites arrived in Rephidim, a place in the wilderness where God told them to camp after their departure from Egypt:

In Exodus 17, the people of Israel were asking [the] question: "Is the Lord with us or not?"

You know why they asked? Because the Lord had told them to leave Egypt. It was the Lord who had made big promises about a promised land. Who had raised up this big-time leader named Moses. Who had produced these big-time plagues in order to free His people from the Egyptians. All for what?

To bring them to the middle of a *desert*?

Verses 1-3 say that it was also the Lord who commanded the Israelites to camp at a place named Rephidim. "Camp" means that you want to be revitalized. You want to sit down and restore your mojo because you've got a long road ahead. The people had their Vitamixes out, hoping to get some juice for the journey. The problem is, God told them to camp where there was no water.

Can you imagine walking from Africa through the Middle East without water? They were in the wilderness, experiencing that dry mouth you get when you eat that honeybun on a July afternoon in Texas but can't find anything to wash it down with— only this was worse. It wasn't some pattycake issue. For them, this was life or death. They had to be thinking, *What? But we're just doing what You said, Lord!*

They were being triple obedient:

- Going in the direction God had called them.
- Following Moses, God's choice to lead them.
- Camping where they were told to camp.

And yet here they were, about to die of thirst.

Many of you have had that disappointment. You thought that if you just slowed down and focused on your marriage, the two of you would get your mojo back. Instead, your relationship is worse. You thought that if you tried that new thing in your business or ministry (the thing you were sure God had green-lighted), the risk would be worth it. But somehow the outlook is still gloomy and gray.

The expectation is what messes you up. The expectation is that if you're camping, *Alright! I'm getting ready for the next phase.* You feel hope for right now and hope for what's ahead. But then you come to the campsite, and you find yourself in a place with no water, about to die of thirst.

Fighting Your Battles, pages 34-35

VIDEO TEACHING NOTES

As you watch the video, use the space below to take notes. Some key points and quotes are provided as reminders.

Main Idea

- Following God doesn't necessarily protect us from life's struggles. We have to spend some time in the dry places, because those dry times build a stronger faith, preparing us for the promised land where God is taking us.

- When we're feeling dehydrated and like we've reached our limit, it's normal to doubt what God is doing and whether He's on our side. Desperate seasons remind us of our delivering God. We won't ever get where He's leading us without exercising faith in Him.

- In the place He's called you is the place where He'll be standing right above you.

- There's a difference between trial and temptation. Though we will sometimes have more trial—more weight and hardship—put on us than we can bear, God will not allow us to be tempted beyond what we can bear. He promises to always provide a way of escape.

- Personal Notes:

Application

Those painful, difficult places that we've followed God to are the places He will provide for us in. He never abandons those who are following Him. But we have to seek Him as our source and provision.

Quotables

- There's a whole lot of pain, a whole lot of burn, just to get prepared for what we were called to do.

- God will pull you into a place that you don't prefer because He wants to make sure that you are ready for that promise.

- Right when God's people were at the precipice of losing faith, as soon as they were about to lose it all, God stepped in and He let them know that He's above it all. God stepped in, put His hands on the weight bar, and started to pull it up to let them know: "Your struggle is not yours alone."

VIDEO GROUP DISCUSSION

1. Jonathan notes that the Israelites in Exodus 17 were faithfully following God; nevertheless, He called them to camp (to rest and reinvigorate) in a place with no water. Desert times like these almost always stir up doubt and fear, and can sometimes make us want to give up on God. Two of the questions that almost every spiritually dehydrated person asks are, "Why did You bring me here, God, when I was following You?" and "Are You with me or not?"

How have you or people you know phrased your questions during times of affliction in the past?

2. Another time in their trek toward the promised land, God's people responded like this:

The whole congregation of the sons of Israel grumbled against Moses and Aaron in the wilderness. The sons of Israel said to them, "If only we had died by the LORD's hand in the land of Egypt, when we sat by the pots of meat, when we ate bread until we were full; for you have brought us out into this wilderness to kill this entire assembly with hunger!"… Moses said, "…The LORD hears your grumblings which you grumble against Him. And what are we? Your grumblings are not against us but against the LORD." (Exodus 16:2-3, 8)

What are some of the accusations the people were really voicing about God?

3. In the video, Jonathan refers to 2 Corinthians 1:8-10, which the apostle Paul wrote in a very transparent letter to the Christians in Corinth. Have someone read this passage out loud.

If Paul—who had endured beatings, imprisonment, mob attacks, hunger, and other hardships and persecution—could feel such despair, what does this tell you about what to expect of your own emotions in times like these?

Reread verses 9 and 10. What was it that allowed Paul to look beyond his emotions?

Comparing the Israelites' response and Paul's, where is the line between expressing our feelings and grumbling against God?

4. What does our time in the "wilderness" do for our faith? From your own experiences and accounts that you've read in the Bible, why does the Lord sometimes lead faithful people into difficulty?

What things do we learn about ourselves in these moments that we aren't likely to learn anywhere else?

What do we learn about God in these seasons that we aren't likely to learn anywhere else?

GROUP BIBLE EXPLORATION

1. Paul urged the young pastor Timothy, "Fight the good fight, keeping faith and a good conscience, which some have rejected and suffered shipwreck in regard to their faith" (1 Timothy 1:18-19). To avoid falling prey to ungodly attitudes and spiritual shipwreck, how can Christians develop a stronger will, a stronger commitment to believe and act in faith when hardships and trials come?

2. Here are a few reactions to suffering seasons that anger God. Read these passages together, and after each one, note the sin or sins involved.

   • Do not forget how you provoked the LORD your God to anger in the wilderness; from the day that you left the land of Egypt until you arrived at this place, you have been rebellious against the LORD. (Deuteronomy 9:7)

   • It came about after the LORD had spoken these words to Job, that the LORD said to Eliphaz the Temanite, "My wrath is kindled against you and against your two friends, because you have not spoken of Me what is trustworthy, as My servant Job has." (Job 42:7)

- "Your forefathers have abandoned Me," declares the LORD, "and have followed other gods…You too have done evil, even more than your forefathers; for behold, each one of you is following the stubbornness of his own evil heart, without listening to Me." (Jeremiah 16:11-12)

3. Have people in the group read each of the following passages out loud. What does God want us to remember in those times when we feel He has abandoned us or hidden Himself from us?

- Isaiah 40:27-29

- Psalm 33:18-20

- 2 Corinthians 1:20

Sometimes faithful people do die, as Jonathan and his family have experienced. Sometimes they do suffer famine or disease or injustice or tragedy in this life. How can God's words still be true?

4. When our friends are enduring a time of despair or depletion, Job 6:14 says, "For the despairing man there should be kindness from his friend; so that he does not abandon the fear of the Almighty." Why is it so important that the person who's suffering "does not abandon [their] fear of the Almighty"?

5. What do these verses say are some of the lasting outcomes for those who faithfully endure thirsty seasons in the wilderness?

- Do not throw away your confidence, which has a great reward. For you have need of endurance, so that when you have done the will of God, you may receive what was promised. (Hebrews 10:35-36)

- Our momentary, light affliction is producing for us an eternal weight of glory far beyond all comparison. (2 Corinthians 4:17)

- Blessed is the man who trusts in the LORD, and whose trust is the LORD. For he will be like a tree planted by the water that extends its roots by a stream, and does not fear when the heat comes; but its leaves will be green, and it will not be anxious in a year of drought, nor cease to yield fruit. (Jeremiah 17:7-8)

What's the difference between trusting "in" the Lord and having the Lord as your "trust"?

What are some ways you can build up both kinds of trust?

IN CLOSING

As you end the study today, pray together for a greater grasp and practice of enduring faith for yourselves and your church. Share about the areas you feel need strengthening in your hearts or minds, especially where the desire, will, and courage to respond in faith are involved. Talk about ways you could encourage each other in this particular part of the journey.

Before Session 3, complete the "On Your Own Between Sessions" section below. You might want to start the next session with participants sharing what they learned from the exercises on these pages.

ON YOUR OWN BETWEEN SESSIONS

1. Where in your life do you feel "dehydrated"—either by an unexpected circumstance or tragedy, by the arrival of yet another obstacle or opponent, or by the same old people problems that never seem to resolve?

   How are you asking God to show up and deliver you or someone you love?

2. The following verses reveal some of the responses God commends when His people are doing what God had called them to do—and yet they're in a season of suffering. Read these passages together and mark the godly response(s) in each situation.

Job

- After four major losses in the course of one day: 1) his work animals and pack animals were carried off by raiders, 2) some of his livestock and servants were killed by lightning, 3) other servants were killed in an enemy attack, and 4) all ten of his adult sons and daughters were killed by a tornado-like wind that collapsed the house they were gathered in:

  Then Job got up, tore his robe, and shaved his head; then he fell to the ground and worshiped. He said, "Naked I came from my mother's womb, and naked I shall return there. The LORD gave and the LORD has taken away. Blessed be the name of the LORD." Despite all this, Job did not sin, nor did he blame God. (Job 1:20-22)

- After Satan afflicted him with severe boils from head to toe:

    Job took a piece of pottery to scrape himself while he was sitting in the ashes. Then his wife said to him, "Do you still hold firm your integrity? Curse God and die!" But he said to her, "You are speaking as one of the foolish women speaks. Shall we actually accept good from God but not accept adversity?" Despite all this, Job did not sin with his lips. (Job 2:8-10)

- After several days or weeks of listening to his friends' assumptions (and sometimes accusations) about God's reasons for letting Job go through all this pain:

    It is still my comfort, and I rejoice in unsparing pain, that I have not denied the words of the Holy One. (Job 6:10)

Jeremiah

- After the Israelites rejected his prophetic words (which were straight from the Lord!) and sought to ruin him personally:

    Heal me, LORD, and I will be healed; save me and I will be saved, for You are my praise. Look, they keep saying to me, "Where is the word of the LORD? Let it come now!" But as for me, I have not hurried away from being a shepherd following after You, nor have I longed for the disastrous day; You Yourself know that the utterance of my lips was in Your presence. Do not be a terror to me; You are my refuge in a day of disaster. Let those who persecute me be put to shame, but as for me, let me not be put to shame; let them be dismayed, but let me not be dismayed. (Jeremiah 17:14-18)

Paul

- Writing from prison after a time of great loneliness and lack of material resources and support:

    I have learned to be content in whatever circumstances I am. I know how to get along with little, and I also know how to live in prosperity; in any and every circumstance I have learned the secret of being filled and going hungry, both of having abundance and suffering need. I can do all things through Him who strengthens me. (Philippians 4:11-12)

Overall, how would you describe the heart, the attitude, the resolve behind these responses?

Which one stands out to you? Why?

3. Looking at Jesus' experience in the garden of Gethsemane in Matthew 26, what do you notice that lets you know that Jesus was feeling the same things that we feel?

> Then Jesus came with them to a place called Gethsemane, and told His disciples, "Sit here while I go over there and pray." And He took Peter and the two sons of Zebedee with Him, and began to be grieved and distressed. Then He said to them, "My soul is deeply grieved, to the point of death; remain here and keep watch with Me." And He went a little beyond *them*, and fell on His face and prayed, saying, "My Father, if it is possible, let this cup pass from Me; yet not as I will, but as You will."
>
> …He went away again a second time and prayed, saying, "My Father, if this cup cannot pass away unless I drink *from* it, Your will be done."
>
> …He…went away and prayed a third time, saying the same thing once more. (Matthew 26:36-39, 42, 44)

Jesus prayed the same words to His Father three separate times. Why do you think He did this?

What does this passage communicate to you about the place of emotions and how to handle them in times like these?

4. Every time Jesus went away to pray, He returned to find the disciples sleeping. Here's what He said to Peter, James, and John the first time: "So, you men could not keep watch with Me for one hour? Keep watching and praying, so that you do not come into temptation; the spirit is willing, but the flesh is weak" (verses 40-41).

   What are the types of temptation that we can easily fall into when we're feeling deep sorrow or distress?

5. Luke 22:43-44 adds these details: "Now an angel from heaven appeared to Him, strengthening Him. And being in agony, He was praying very fervently; and His sweat became like drops of blood, falling down upon the ground." List some of the other ways that God ministers to His people in their agony and desperation.

   How has He ministered to you—broken through for you as the Living Water—in your place with no water?

RECOMMENDED READING

In preparation for Session 3, please read chapters 4–6 in *Fighting Your Battles* by Jonathan Evans.

FIGHTING GOD'S WAY

Here's another excerpt from *Fighting Your Battles*, where Jonathan shares a very personal moment in the life of his family that illustrates our need for a spiritual perspective in order to fight God's way.

> If you're only battling in the physical realm, without a spiritual perspective, then you may be battling in the right place…but you're not operating *from* the right place. We have to learn to operate from the top, because [Exodus 17] says that when Moses held up the staff [in the battle against the Amalekites], Joshua gained victory in the valley.
>
> In that hotel room on the day my parents broke the news to us kids about my mom's cancer, Mom was sitting there taking in everyone's reaction, and the first words out of her mouth were Scripture, a paraphrase of Ephesians 6:12: "Y'all know that this fight is not against flesh and blood. This fight is against the principalities and powers and forces of darkness that war in heavenly places. The enemy is attacking, so we need to fight."
>
> Many of you are dealing with health issues. You're dealing with financial issues. You're dealing with relational or parenting issues, or addiction issues. Regardless of the battle you're in, it's a spiritual battle above all. There are things going on in the supernatural realm—forces beyond what your eyes can see—that are actively working to defeat you, even destroy you. The battle is your opportunity to pull down the power of heaven to overcome what's coming at you on earth.
>
> The call has to come from the top, and then it gets executed at the bottom. This is what I learned from playing football my whole life…The ones who win are the ones who get their plays from above.
>
> When we recognize that every earthly battle is part of the spiritual war, it changes

our perspective. We let the Lord have the lead. We let God decide the battle plan and guide us to victory. And we never have to back down.

With Him in charge, we can take over situations that would like to overtake us. With Him in charge, we can overcome what tries to come over us.

Fighting Your Battles, pages 61-62

VIDEO TEACHING NOTES

As you watch the video, use the space below to take notes. Some key points and quotes are provided as reminders.

Main Idea

- There is a way to fight, and it's not our way. Fighting God's way means taking responsibility in the battle as God calls us, but realizing that the battle is really the Lord's. He's the owner of it; we're the stewards.

- The spiritual realm is where earth's battles are won. The spiritual realm has authority over the physical realm. Most of us want to fight in the physical and forget the spiritual, but when we're fighting, we're not fighting against flesh and blood. It's a fight that's much higher than we think. The call has to come from the top, and then it gets executed at the bottom.

- We have to be responsible with what we're going through, but we can't forget about prayer as we go through it. To pray at all times is important for the victory, because that's how we connect to heaven from our position on earth. It's how we let the Lord lead, acknowledging that we cannot win on our own. It's how we make sure that we're partnering with God, not replacing God.

- Though one of the hardest things about trusting God is waiting on Him for the victory, we don't have to be afraid to wait. That's where our strength is renewed. And what helps us wait, what helps us hold up the spiritual perspective and be good stewards of our responsibilities and commitments, is refusing to go it alone.

- Looking to the Lord in our battles is critical. Fighting His way is essential. But there is power in the community of believers too. The family of God is there to hold our hands up when the burden starts to get too heavy.

- Personal Notes:

Application

We can't handle the burden of battle alone. God is the owner; we are the stewards. So to fight His way means looking to heaven, relying on God to lead us to victory as we execute our assignments here on earth.

Quotables

- A lot of times we realize through our frustration that we just stepped into God's territory, that we're trying to take His position in our problem. And we realize quickly that we need to surrender the battle to God. We realize real quickly that the battle is not even ours.

- The spiritual perspective and the spiritual realm is really what helps you defeat the physical realm.

- If all you see is what you see, you do not see all there is to be seen. There is a spiritual battle behind the physical presence that you're facing.

- We have to bring God in. We have to let Him know that we really believe prayer works when we work in prayer.

- The trick of the enemy is to make you think you need to carry the ball to the end zone by yourself, knowing that he has an army that's waiting to tackle you on every try. Listen to me. You are not alone.

- Waiting is important—a test of your faith—to show that you really trust God with this battle that actually belongs to Him.

VIDEO GROUP DISCUSSION

1. When we experience hard things, says Jonathan, what we want to do is "fight our way—anything we can do to relieve the pressure, anything we can do to make sure everything is better." We use human logic to try to solve a divine problem, and then we wonder why we have none of the divine peace or rest that Jesus promised.

    What are some of the human solutions and pressure relievers that people often turn to in their battles in place of God?

There *is* a time and place for helpful resources, but we need to turn to heaven first, because as Jonathan discusses throughout this entire session, God is the owner of our battles.

2. What are the different functions between an owner and a steward (manager) when it comes to operating a successful business? How and when do they coordinate and partner together?

Now apply this to the battlefield. How do we keep from taking God's position in our problems? How can we actively let Him own our battles without neglecting our "duties" as stewards?

3. We never know whether the Lord will ask us to partner with Him in the battle, as He did with Moses and Joshua in Exodus 17, or whether He will outright fight and win the victory for us, as He did for His people in 2 Chronicles 20. What remains true at all times, says Jonathan, is that we must look to Him and wait on Him.

On average, *how often* do you wait on God for strategies and instruction when you're in the middle of a battle, rather than just forging ahead with your own plans?

How well would you say you wait on Him? Explain your answer.

What's the hardest part for you about waiting on Him?

4. We often feel like waiting weakens us, but God says otherwise: "Those who wait for the LORD will gain new strength" (Isaiah 40:31). In what ways does waiting actually strengthen us?

How could you develop your trust and your ability to wait when you're away from the battle?

GROUP BIBLE EXPLORATION

1. Second Corinthians 10:3-4 is a foundational passage for the entire teaching in this session: "Though we walk in the flesh, we do not wage battle according to the flesh, for the weapons of our warfare are not of the flesh, but divinely powerful for the destruction of fortresses." According to the following passages, what are some of the indicators of a person who is battling God's way and not according to the flesh? Sum them up in your own words.

- We are afflicted in every way, but not crushed; perplexed, but not despairing; persecuted, but not abandoned; struck down, but not destroyed; always carrying around in the body the dying of Jesus, so that the life of Jesus may also be revealed in our body…Therefore we do not lose heart, but though our outer person is decaying, yet our inner person is being renewed day by day. (2 Corinthians 4:8-10, 16)

- They seek Me day by day and delight to know My ways, as a nation that has done righteousness and has not forsaken the ordinance of their God. They ask Me for just decisions, they delight in the nearness of God. (Isaiah 58:2)

- The LORD was with Jehoshaphat because he…sought the God of his father, followed

His commandments, and did not act as Israel did…He took great pride in the ways of the LORD. (2 Chronicles 17:3, 6)

- Our conscience testifies that we have conducted ourselves in the world, and especially in our relations with you, with integrity and godly sincerity. We have done so, relying not on worldly wisdom but on God's grace. (2 Corinthians 1:12 NIV)

And don't forget…Because Christianity is "a team sport," as Jonathan calls it, these are also characteristics of the people you should have fighting alongside you!

2. Jonathan referred to Ephesians 6:18, "Pray at all times in the Spirit," as a practical way for us to stay connected to heaven during our earthly battles. Read each of the following verses together to discover some additional ways we can maintain a spiritual perspective at all times.

- Do not be conformed to this world, but be transformed by the renewing of your mind, so that you may prove what the will of God is, that which is good and acceptable and perfect. (Romans 12:2)

- Trust in the LORD with all your heart, and do not lean on your own understanding. In all your ways acknowledge him, and he will make straight your paths. (Proverbs 3:5-6 ESV)

- We demolish arguments and every pretension that sets itself up against the knowledge of God, and we take captive every thought to make it obedient to Christ. (2 Corinthians 10:5 NIV)

- If you have been raised with Christ, keep seeking the things that are above, where Christ is, seated at the right hand of God. Set your minds on the things that are above, not on the things that are on earth. (Colossians 3:1-2)

Which of these disciplines presents the biggest ongoing challenge to you? Why?

3. What are some of the battle advantages of looking to the Lord? Mark those in the verses below.

- The angel of the LORD encamps around those who fear Him, and rescues them… They who seek the LORD will not lack any good thing. (Psalm 34:7, 10)

- Do you not know? Have you not heard? The Everlasting God, the LORD, the Creator of the ends of the earth does not become weary or tired. His understanding is unsearchable. He gives strength to the weary, and to the one who lacks might He increases power. (Isaiah 40:28-29)

- The eyes of the LORD are toward the righteous, and His ears are toward their cry for help…The righteous cry out, and the LORD hears and rescues them from all their troubles. The LORD is near to the brokenhearted and saves those who are crushed in spirit. (Psalm 34:15, 17-18)

What advantages have you experienced by seeking the Lord rather than trying to go it alone?

4. Ephesians 6:12-13 reminds us of the real enemy and what our main responsibilities are as God's stewards in the battle: "Our struggle is not against flesh and blood, but against the rulers, against the powers, against the world forces of this darkness, against the spiritual forces of wickedness in the heavenly places. Therefore, take up the full armor of God, so that you will be able to resist on the evil day, and having done everything, to stand firm."

List the three primary responsibilities of every Christian that are mentioned here, and then share what practices or disciplines have helped you faithfully carry them out when the battle was raging.

   1.

   2.

   3.

What additional ideas have you gained from this session for spiritual strengthening and spiritual awareness?

IN CLOSING

As you end the study today, pray as a group for the Lord to continue to open your eyes to the spiritual realm, not only within your earthly battles but as you carry out your day-to-day responsibilities. Pray that His Spirit will continue to train you to draw on the power of heaven constantly and to look to God for help instinctively. And in whatever battle you're facing right now, thank the Lord for owning it so you don't have to. Then ask Him to give you strategic guidance and support for this fight.

Before Session 4, complete the "On Your Own Between Sessions" section below.

ON YOUR OWN BETWEEN SESSIONS

1. Psalm 37:1-9 speaks of several common reactions to our enemies and possible responses toward God. Mark the parts of this passage that accurately describe you at this point in your life.

> Do not get upset because of evildoers,
> Do not be envious of wrongdoers.
> For they will wither quickly like the grass,
> And decay like the green plants.
> Trust in the LORD and do good;
> Live in the land and cultivate faithfulness.
> Delight yourself in the LORD;
> And He will give you the desires of your heart.
> Commit your way to the LORD,
> Trust also in Him, and He will do it.
> He will bring out your righteousness as the light,
> And your judgment as the noonday.
> Rest in the LORD and wait patiently for Him;
> Do not get upset because of one who is successful in his way,
> Because of the person who carries out wicked schemes.
> Cease from anger and abandon wrath;
> Do not get upset; it leads only to evildoing.

For evildoers will be eliminated,
But those who wait for the LORD, they will inherit the land.

Of all the excellent commands seen here, write out in the space below the specific statements that you really feel led to focus on right now. What ideas is the Lord giving you that would help train you in these areas?

2. After each of the following passages, sum up why it's important that we get our instructions and strategies for earth's battles from above.

- It is He who sits above the circle of the earth, and its inhabitants are like grasshoppers...It is He who reduces rulers to nothing, who makes the judges of the earth meaningless...He merely blows on them, and they wither, and the storm carries them away like stubble. "To whom then will you compare Me that I would be his equal?" says the Holy One. Raise your eyes on high and see who has created these stars, the One who brings out their multitude by number, He calls them all by name; because of the greatness of His might and the strength of His power, not one of them is missing. (Isaiah 40:22-26)

- The LORD nullifies the plan of nations; He frustrates the plans of peoples. The plan of the LORD stands forever, the plans of His heart from generation to generation. (Psalm 33:10-11)

- We have this treasure in earthen containers, so that the extraordinary greatness of the power will be of God and not from ourselves. (2 Corinthians 4:7)

- [Jesus prayed,] "Our Father, who is in heaven, hallowed be Your name. Your kingdom come. Your will be done, on earth as it is in heaven." (Matthew 6:9-10)

3. Who are your Aaron and Hur—the fellow believers who prayerfully support you in the battle and keep urging you to live faithfully in the Lord? What have you learned from each of those people about how to help bear someone else's burden?

Whose name has God put on your heart who's needing some extra support and encouragement right now? How could you specifically help hold up their arms in *their* battle until they see the victory?

How do we strike the right balance between leaning on others…but not too much? Leaning on others yet relying on God above all?

4. Here's a word from Jonathan, from page 64 of his book, for those times when we're tempted to run from the battle because it seems too much for us:

> Never lose sight of the mountaintop, friend. And don't quit on your earthly responsibilities either. Even though it's difficult…be faithful in your marriage. Do your work well. Keep your promises to your kids. And take care of your relationships

and your finances and your commitments. Then you'll see God come through like He came through for Joshua, Moses, and ultimately the people of Israel.

My mom looked to God during her battle with cancer, *and* she acted responsibly. She went to the doctor. Followed medical protocol. Went on a strict diet with all the sugars removed (because sugar feeds cancer cells). She fought *and* she believed God's Word. She did, and we did as a family.

And we won.

How did we win, you ask? I mean, my mom did die of cancer after a great fight.

Well, if we could hear her now, I'm sure she would say, "I won big. If only you could see what I see."

You may not win the way you think you will, or the way you pray to win. But God has victory in store for those who trust Him.

In what area of your life do you need to be more faithful? Write a prayer of confession and renewed commitment to God here.

5. As further reminders for yourself and your own life, what can you take away from these prophetic words to Judah's king Asa and the people of God?

- Listen to me, Asa, and all Judah and Benjamin: the LORD is with you when you are with Him. And if you seek Him, He will let you find Him. (2 Chronicles 15:2)

- Were not the Ethiopians and the Lubim an immense army with very many chariots and horsemen? Yet because you relied on the LORD, He handed them over to you. For the eyes of the LORD roam throughout the earth, so that He may strongly support those whose heart is completely His. (2 Chronicles 16:8-9)

RECOMMENDED READING

In preparation for Session 4, please read chapters 7–8 in *Fighting Your Battles* by Jonathan Evans.

FROM SAFE TO FAITH

In this excerpt from *Fighting Your Battles*, Jonathan uses the disciples' experience on the Sea of Galilee in Matthew 14 to counter what we typically think when we find our boat—and our beliefs—being battered by a storm:

> Let me tell you something about the trials and tribulations of life. When you're doing everything you can to get yourself out of difficulty but you're getting no movement away from the difficulty, it's probably because God has put you in it. We know that rough times are sometimes the result of disobedience, but not every time. The faithful also face resistance.
>
> In their obedience, the disciples were experiencing contrary winds. Forceful winds that were pushing back at them. While in the will of God, they found themselves straining at the oars in a boat that was being battered by waves. Sometimes it's not until you follow Jesus that you hit the really rough waters.
>
> This is a big reason for making sure that you obey—and build confidence in your obedience. Then you won't be so quick to conclude, "I'm not in God's will," just because things are rocky in your marriage or your job or with your kids.
>
> The rains may be soaking you. Your world may feel unstable. You may be a long distance from land, where you're being tossed around and tormented by circumstances. *And yet you may be in the exact center of God's will.* For the obedient one, the contrary winds and bashing waves can be evidence of your faithfulness.
>
> At another time, Jesus warned His disciples, "'A slave is not greater than his master.' If they persecuted Me, they will persecute you as well" (John 15:20). As with Jesus' own life, you can be obedient…and your obedience may carry you right into resistance.

When you follow God, doing what He asks of you, your storm may be a sign of your commitment and calling. A sign that you are His and He is yours.

That's what's here in the Scriptures. If you're encountering contrary winds in your calling from God, you'd best believe He is preparing you for a commission that is contrary to the world's calling. In fact, once you decide to row against the currents of culture and live for Him, that's when you can expect to experience the *most* resistance! All these things coming against you probably mean you're being called to go against these things.

The good news is, God will push you through the very circumstance He's put you in. If He is your "problem," only He can be your solution. If He is the one who brought you here, He's the one who's going to get you out.

Fighting Your Battles, pages 130-131

VIDEO TEACHING NOTES

As you watch the video, use the space below to take notes. Some key points and quotes are provided as reminders.

Main Idea

- When we're facing contrary winds while doing what God has called us to do, it's because God wants us to be ready to face the contrary winds that will come with the future that He will call us to.

- By walking on the water in the middle of a storm, Jesus was letting His disciples know: He was on top of the chaos, reigning supreme over their problem. And that lets us know: Our problems are not bigger than our Savior, but we need to come to our Savior in our problems.

- We are often afraid of the very thing that has the power to save us. Sometimes in a storm, the truth looks like a distortion. But it's not the truth that's the distortion, it's our view because of what we're going through.

- Peter put the truth to the test, and so can we. Because if it's really true, we should be able to do something with the truth that we could never do without it.

- Faith is not a feeling. Faith has to do with your feet and what your feet are willing to do in spite of your feelings.

- Personal Notes:

Application

Jesus is in the storm with you, but you have to come to Him. He has already come and done His part—He's already walked on the chaos. Now you have to do your part. Stop thinking about your failures and your fear, and step toward the truth. Jesus is saying, "No matter what you're going through, I have one word for you: *Come.*"

Quotables

- In your obedience, there are going to be contrary winds because your calling is contrary to most things.

- Peter made a decision that all of us have to make when we hit a storm. We all have to realize that God is calling us to press through contrary winds—and when we get the most discouraged, come to Jesus.

- Come. Don't go farther from Jesus in the storm. Come to Him in the storm.

- How do you know if the truth is the truth in the middle of a storm? You apply God's Word and see if it allows you to do something you couldn't do without it.

VIDEO GROUP DISCUSSION

1. Jonathan opens this session with the reminder that obeying Jesus doesn't keep you from facing contrary winds. In fact, sometimes following Him means you end up in the middle of a monster storm. Yet we should expect contrary winds in the course of our faith because our calling is contrary to most things.

   How do you tend to react when a sudden storm in life comes your way?

   Where do your thoughts usually go about the reasons for your difficulty? What assumptions do you typically make about your standing with God?

2. The disciples thought Jesus—the Truth who was coming right at them—was a ghost because of how storms distort our vision. What kinds of things tend to affect how we view the truth in the middle of the chaos?

3. In difficult times, says Jonathan, people often start thinking that there's something wrong with the truth, that it's something they need to run from. So they'll ignore the Bible, skip out on church, refuse accountability...

What's been your experience? When you've felt like this, how have you tried to run from the truth? Or what have you seen others do?

How did that response affect your faith (or that person's faith)?

4. Peter put truth to the test. He was scared, but he moved his feet and came to Jesus, and as a result, he was able to experience the truth and overcome something he could never have overcome on his own. When was the last time you obeyed and came to Jesus in the middle of a storm, even though you were afraid?

What was your motivator for that decision?

What happened? What changed, what did you overcome, by stepping out in faith?

GROUP BIBLE EXPLORATION

1. Read the following passages out loud. They speak of sudden storms and terrifying times in life when we may initially have trouble seeing God. What do you learn from these verses about how to handle those times?

   - Proverbs 3:25-26

   - Psalm 31:21-24

   - 1 Peter 3:16-18

2. Read the scriptures below and first write down the reality that we're warned of—that we shouldn't be surprised of. Next, write down the outcome, the reward, of having faith in Jesus during storms and trials.

   - Consider it all joy, my brothers and sisters, when you encounter various trials, knowing that the testing of your faith produces endurance. And let endurance have its perfect result, so that you may be perfect and complete, lacking in nothing. (James 1:2-4)

     The Reality:

     The Reward(s):

   - For this is the love of God, that we keep His commandments; and His commandments are not burdensome. For whoever has been born of God overcomes the world; and this is the victory that has overcome the world: our faith. Who is the one who overcomes the world, but the one who believes that Jesus is the Son of God? (1 John 5:3-5)

> *The Reality:*

> *The Reward(s):*

- Even though I walk through the valley of the shadow of death, I fear no evil, for You are with me. (Psalm 23:4)

> *The Reality:*

> *The Reward(s):*

- Just as the sufferings of Christ are ours in abundance, so also our comfort is abundant through Christ. (2 Corinthians 1:5)

> *The Reality:*

> *The Reward(s):*

What are some of the sufferings of Christ that we can expect to endure?

3. What reassurances do you find in these verses for those who willingly approach God in their time of weakness?

- If any of you lacks wisdom, let him ask of God, who gives to all generously and without reproach, and it will be given to him. But he must ask in faith without any doubting, for the one who doubts is like the surf of the sea, driven and tossed by the wind. (James 1:5-6)

- Beloved, if our heart does not condemn us, we have confidence before God; and whatever we ask, we receive from Him, because we keep His commandments and do the things that are pleasing in His sight. This is His commandment, that we believe in the name of His Son Jesus Christ, and love one another, just as He commanded us. (1 John 3:21-23)

- Know that the LORD has set apart the godly person for Himself; the LORD hears when I call to Him. Tremble, and do not sin; meditate in your heart upon your bed, and be still. *Offer the sacrifices of righteousness,* and trust in the LORD. (Psalm 4:3-5)

- "Because of the groaning of the needy, Now I will arise," says the LORD; "I will put him in the safety for which he longs." (Psalm 12:5)

IN CLOSING

As you end your time together, encourage one another to come to Jesus no matter how bad your individual storms might be. Openly share about any fears or hesitations you may have, and take some time to pray over those in the group whose faith is wavering.

Before Session 5, complete the "On Your Own Between Sessions" section below.

ON YOUR OWN BETWEEN SESSIONS

1. Recall a time when the truth was right in front of you, but you missed it. What was going on inside of you that blinded you to it?

2. Which emotions tend to most typically distort your perception of the truth in the middle of a storm?

Explore the book of Psalms for a couple of passages that counteract and "speak truth" to those emotions. Write the verses here so you can refer to them the next time your distorting emotions surface.

3. Read the following passages from the book of Hebrews and, after each one, write down what type of heart the Lord does or does not respond to. (Some passages will have more than one answer.)

- Let's approach God with a sincere heart in full assurance of faith, having our hearts sprinkled clean from an evil conscience and our bodies washed with pure water. Let's hold firmly to the confession of our hope without wavering, for He who promised is faithful. (10:22-23)

- As the Holy Spirit says, "Today if you hear His voice, do not harden your hearts as when [My people] provoked Me, as on the day of trial in the wilderness, where your fathers put Me to the test, and saw My works for forty years. Therefore I was angry with this generation, and said, 'They always go astray in their heart, and they did not know My ways;...They certainly shall not enter My rest.'" (3:7-11)

- Take care, brothers and sisters, that there will not be in any one of you an evil, unbelieving heart that falls away from the living God. But encourage one another every day, as long as it is still called "today," so that none of you will be hardened by the deceitfulness of sin. For we have become partakers of Christ if we keep the beginning of our commitment firm until the end. (3:12-14)

From the passages above, list the consequences of a disobedient heart.

What are some further consequences you've seen in your own life or other people's lives?

What are the blessings of an obedient heart?

4. Hebrews 12:1-2 says this: "Since we…have such a great cloud of witnesses surrounding us, let's rid ourselves of every obstacle and the sin which so easily entangles us, and let's run with endurance the race that is set before us, looking only at Jesus, the originator and perfecter of the faith." Besides the state of our heart, what are some of the other things that can trip us up and prevent us from coming to Jesus?

How does it help knowing that so many Christians who have preceded us, including Jesus Himself, have successfully endured the storms and run the race?

5. Put your faith into practice. What comfort zone—what seemingly safe place—is Jesus calling you out of right now? How willing are you to come to Him? Explain your answer.

If you're having trouble taking that step of faith, read what Paul prayed for the Christians in Ephesus:

I keep asking that the God of our Lord Jesus Christ, the glorious Father, may give you the Spirit of wisdom and revelation, so that you may know him better. I pray that the eyes of your heart may be enlightened in order that you may know the hope to which he has called you, the riches of his glorious inheritance in his holy people, and his incomparably great power for us who believe. That power is the same as the mighty strength he exerted when he raised Christ from the dead and seated him at his right hand in the heavenly realms, far above all rule and authority, power and dominion, and every name that is invoked, not only in the present age but also in the one to come. (Ephesians 1:17-21 NIV)

What godly hope, what glorious riches, what greatness do you need to have the eyes of your heart opened to?

Pray this over yourself today, personalizing the wording: "I ask that *You*, *God*, may give *me* the Spirit of wisdom and revelation, so that *I* may know Him better…"

RECOMMENDED READING

In preparation for Session 5, please read chapters 9–11 in *Fighting Your Battles* by Jonathan Evans.

PREPARE FOR THE FORECAST

I n this excerpt from *Fighting Your Battles*, Jonathan shares about what Jesus has said and done to make sure we know what it takes to build strong for the bad weather to come:

> Jesus was warning [in Luke 6:46] that you can't have it your way and His way. Either He is your all in all or He isn't. If Jesus is your all in all, then He is Lord and Captain, Master and King. He is Lord of your life, Captain of your ship, the Master you serve, and the King over your kingdom. You work for Him and you build by His rules. His method seems harsh until you learn His motive: "If anyone loves Me," explained Jesus, "he will follow My word; and My Father will love him, and We will come to him and make Our dwelling with him" (John 14:23).
>
> Remember, Jesus knows what's coming our way, and He's forewarned us because He loves us. He knows what's necessary to survive the strongest winds, and He's given us the master plan, a plan that fits the Father's specifications for protecting us. Jesus has walked the way of the Servant Himself. He lived what He preached, coming to earth and carrying out His Father's instructions from start to finish. His true followers reveal themselves in the same way: by not only following His lead but following His commands.
>
> Do you want to know the life God blesses? Do you want to have a life that makes you unshakable? Do you want a house that won't fail at the first storm that comes along? Listen to your Lord. Commit to your King. The servant's life is built on solid ground.
>
> *Fighting Your Battles*, pages 160-161

VIDEO TEACHING NOTES

As you watch the video, use the space below to take notes. Some key points and quotes are provided as reminders.

Main Idea

- If you're not in a difficult season right now, you will be soon. Your faith is going to be tested to see if it will stand. Those words aren't to scare us but to prepare us, so that we're building our lives and our faith on solid rock.

- We must build our foundation now, before the storm comes, making sure our blueprint is based on God's Word.

- Storms make us susceptible, they make us feel vulnerable, but also, they reveal where we really stand and what we're building on. They make it evident who we serve and who we trust: ourselves or the Lord.

- It's not enough to build on God's Word. We have to operate by it, doing what it says even when it says things we don't like. There will be times when acting on it makes us feel vulnerable in the battle, but our vulnerability creates a vacancy. A vacancy that gives God room to maneuver so that victory can be won.

- Personal Notes:

Application

It's time to prepare for the forecast now, not later. Because your faith *is* going to be tested. And the one whose house will still be standing rock-solid after the storm is the one who has built on God's Word and who acts on God's Word.

Quotables

- The difference between a foundation of rock and a foundation of sand is simple: the rock is God's Word, the sand is man's word, man's perspective, man's feelings about a matter.

- Wise men want to build a house, and fools want to build a house. The only way you can distinguish between a wise man and a fool is when a storm shows up.

- You cannot fix a foundation in the middle of a storm. All construction ceases when the storm shows up.

- A lot of Christians have totally lost their fizz because they've been sitting too long. They're not applying God's Word, and therefore their foundation is not being solidified.

- Are you operating in God's Word even when it doesn't feel right? Because even though it doesn't feel right, you'll come to realize quickly: it *is* right.

VIDEO GROUP DISCUSSION

1. Jonathan opens this session by sharing about a question that people have often asked after all the losses he and his family have endured in the past few years: "How in the world are you still standing?" His answer: "It all boils down to a foundation that was constructed way before the storm showed up"—a foundation of weekly devotions in God's Word around the family dinner table.

   Did your family (whether Christian or not) have any foundational habits or traditions that grounded you while you were growing up, either as a person or in your faith? What were they, and how have they helped you stand strong in rough weather?

2. James 1:22 commands us to be doers of the Word, not just hearers. This is essential to building a strong foundation. Too many people, though, try to skip this step.

   As Jonathan describes it, being a *hearer only* is like a Coke or Sprite that's been sitting too long—you lose your fizz, your spiritual vibrancy. What are some other things a person loses, or even misses out on, when they only listen to the Word but don't act on it?

   Another problem with losing your fizz, according to Jonathan, is that you become luke-warm. What's God's response to lukewarm faith, according to Revelation 3:15-16?

Why do you think the Lord would prefer even a cold heart over a lukewarm one?

3. Later in the video, Jonathan cites Joshua's second battle against Ai as an example of hearing and following God's commands even when God's plan doesn't make sense to our sensibilities. God wanted Joshua and a few thousand of his men to pretend they were losing and run from the entrance of the city of Ai so that once Ai's men were lured away, the rest of Israel's army could ambush Ai from a different direction.

When has the Holy Spirit ever directed you to step back so that God could step in?

How did that instruction make you feel at first?

If you did what God said—in spite of your instincts, and how you felt about it, and what it looked like to others—how did your willingness to be vulnerable to God's Word confuse your enemy and make them vulnerable?

4. Besides what it does to the enemy, what are some other good reasons for getting out of God's way and letting Him win our battles however He wants to?

GROUP BIBLE EXPLORATION

1. Too many Christians are Christians in name only. Their religion looks good on the out-
   side—they go to church, attend Bible studies, and listen to the sermons—but they've
   built on sand. It's all just a façade. Disciples are the wise man in the parable in Matthew
   14. They build on an unshakable foundation: the rock of God's Word and our corner-
   stone, the living Word, Jesus Christ.

   What were some of the specific things you tried to build your life on before you met Christ?

2. Disciples are also doers, not just hearers. Here's an analogy Jonathan gave in the book
   (pages 163-164):

   > No coach asks his players to just come and listen. He asks them to get on the field
   > and run the plays, and if they can't do that, there's going to be a problem. If a coach
   > expects his players to show up and do what they've heard, then why would Jesus
   > Christ's expectations be any less in His kingdom? Don't just go to church and be
   > satisfied with listening. Get to work! Dig deep and do as He tells you!…He knows
   > what it takes to construct a house that will still be standing after the storm has passed.

   > The Head Coach in heaven isn't invested in players who just like to sit on the bench.
   > If they don't care about executing on the field, His attitude will be, *Yeah, that's not
   > someone I can use for My kingdom. They aren't interested in winning, and they really
   > don't care about the game plan.*

   > The fundamental question is, will you execute? Once you come to Jesus, and you
   > hear His words, will you do them?

   > This is the difference between a Christian and a disciple. A Christian believes in
   > Jesus. A disciple believes *and* follows Jesus with his or her actions and decisions.
   > You can look at a true disciple's life and know that this person believes in Jesus with-
   > out them saying a word. "Christians," on the other hand, often have to tell you or
   > you wouldn't ever know.

   What are some other distinctives that separate disciples of Christ from those who simply
   claim Christ?

3. God's commands aren't just obligations. He rewards our obedience in many ways. Read these scriptures together and sum up in your own words the blessings of following Him that are promised.

- I have set the LORD continually before me; because He is at my right hand, I will not be shaken. Therefore my heart is glad and my glory rejoices; my flesh also will dwell securely… You will make known to me the way of life; in Your presence is fullness of joy; in Your right hand there are pleasures forever. (Psalm 16:8-9, 11)

- Do not forget my teaching, but let your heart keep my commandments, for length of days and years of life and peace they will add to you. (Proverbs 3:1-2 ESV)

- My son, do not let wisdom and understanding out of your sight, preserve sound judgment and discretion; they will be life for you, an ornament to grace your neck. Then you will go on your way in safety, and your foot will not stumble. When you lie down, you will not be afraid; when you lie down, your sleep will be sweet. (Proverbs 3:21-24 NIV)

What does "an ornament to grace your neck" make you think of? Discuss what this imagery might mean.

Share one way that God has personally blessed your obedience.

4. How do these scriptural assurances of the steadfastness of God's Word encourage you as you continue to build your life in Christ? Read each one out loud.

- Psalm 12:6-7

- Psalm 145:13

- Isaiah 40:8

What do these truths say to you about God's character?

IN CLOSING

As you wrap up your time together, remind each other that while storms will come, we don't have to dread them. Pray for each other to continue to build on the Rock of Christ, and to be faithful in your preparations. And for those who may need to step back so that God's plan can step forward, ask Him for greater faith to trust His power, His timing, His path to victory.

ON YOUR OWN BETWEEN SESSIONS

1. In this session we've seen that those who withstand the storms and win the battles are able to do so because they not only build on the right foundation, but they obey what God says, following His time frame and trusting His methods no matter how unorthodox or uncomfortable that battle plan might be. Those who fall are those who fail to do what God has specified.

First Samuel 15 recounts a telling incident in King Saul's life where he showed his true colors and lost big. Read these excerpts from his story and then answer the questions.

Samuel said to Saul, "The LORD sent me to anoint you as king over His people, over Israel; now therefore, listen to the words of the LORD. This is what the LORD of armies says: 'I will punish Amalek for what he did to Israel…Now go and strike Amalek and completely destroy everything that he has, and do not spare him; but put to death both man and woman, child and infant, ox and sheep, camel and donkey.'"

…Saul defeated the Amalekites…He captured Agag the king of the Amalekites alive, and completely destroyed all the people with the edge of the sword. But Saul and the people spared Agag and the best of the sheep, the oxen, the more valuable animals, the lambs, and everything that was good, and were unwilling to destroy them completely; but everything despicable and weak, that they completely destroyed.

Then the word of the LORD came to Samuel, saying, "I regret that I have made Saul king, because he has turned back from following Me and has not carried out My commands." And Samuel was furious and cried out to the LORD all night. Samuel got up early in the morning to meet Saul…and Saul said to him, "Blessed are you of the LORD! I have carried out the command of the LORD." But Samuel said, "What then is this bleating of the sheep in my ears, and the bellowing of the oxen which I hear?…The LORD sent you on a mission, and said, 'Go and completely destroy the sinners, the Amalekites, and fight against them until they are eliminated.' Why then did you not obey the voice of the LORD?…"

Then Saul said to Samuel, "I did obey the voice of the LORD, for I went on the mission on which the LORD sent me; and I have brought Agag the king of Amalek, and have completely destroyed the Amalekites. But the people took some of the spoils, sheep and oxen, the choicest of the things designated for destruction, to sacrifice to the LORD your God at Gilgal."…[Samuel said,] "Since you have rejected the word of the LORD, He has also rejected you from being king." (verses 1-3, 7-14, 18-21, 23)

What excuses and tactics does Saul use to try to justify his disobedience?

Why do you think the Lord went so far as to take away Saul's throne? Samuel's words to Saul provide some insight:

Samuel said, "Does the LORD have as much delight in burnt offerings and sacrifices as in obeying the voice of the LORD? Behold, to obey is better than a sacrifice, and to pay attention is better than the fat of rams. For rebellion is as reprehensible as the sin of divination, and insubordination is as reprehensible as false religion and idolatry." (verses 22-23)

We're usually so focused on whether we can trust God, that we forget: God wants to be able to trust us too. What did Saul's decisions here indicate about his character, his faith, and the strength of his foundation?

2. How do we build on the rock? What are some of the things that God says make you unshakable? Read the following passages and, after each one, write down those qualities or practices that will help you build wisely so that you can stand firm and complete your mission.

- Be diligent to present yourself approved to God as a worker who does not need to be ashamed, accurately handling the word of truth. But avoid worldly and empty chatter, for it will lead to further ungodliness… If anyone cleanses himself from these things, he will be an implement for honor, sanctified, useful to the Master, prepared for every good work. Now flee from youthful lusts and pursue righteousness, faith, love, and peace with those who call on the Lord from a pure heart. (2 Timothy 2:15-16, 21-22)

- Brothers and sisters, since we have confidence to enter the holy place by the blood of Jesus,…let's approach God with a sincere heart in full assurance of faith, having our hearts sprinkled clean from an evil conscience and our bodies washed with pure water. Let's hold firmly to the confession of our hope without wavering, for He who promised is faithful; and let's consider how to encourage one another in love and good deeds, not abandoning our own meeting together, as is the habit of some people, but encouraging one another; and all the more as you see the day drawing near. (Hebrews 10:19, 22-24)

What do these first two passages also indicate about the impact of having friends in the faith?

- A prudent person sees evil and hides himself, but the naive proceed, and pay the penalty. The reward of humility and the fear of the LORD are riches, honor, and life. Thorns and snares are in the way of the perverse; one who guards himself will be far from them. (Proverbs 22:3-5)

- My soul, wait in silence for God alone, for my hope is from Him. He alone is my rock and my salvation, my refuge; I will not be shaken. My salvation and my glory rest on God; the rock of my strength, my refuge is in God. Trust in Him at all times, you people; pour out your hearts before Him; God is a refuge for us. (Psalm 62:5-8)

- As you have received Christ Jesus the Lord, so walk in Him, having been firmly rooted and now being built up in Him and established in your faith, just as you were instructed, and overflowing with gratitude. (Colossians 2:6-7)

- You, beloved, building yourselves up on your most holy faith, praying in the Holy Spirit, keep yourselves in the love of God, looking forward to the mercy of our Lord Jesus Christ to eternal life. (Jude 19-21)

- Finally, brothers and sisters, whatever is true, whatever is honorable, whatever is right, whatever is pure, whatever is lovely, whatever is commendable, if there is any excellence and if anything worthy of praise, think about these things. (Philippians 4:8)

What are other biblical practices or qualities that have grounded you firmly?

3. Philippians 2:15-16 urges, "Prove yourselves to be blameless and innocent, children of God above reproach in the midst of a crooked and perverse generation, among whom you appear as lights in the world, holding firmly the word of life."

Where in your life are you especially "holding firmly the word of life"? How are you doing this?

4. Jonathan drew on his recall of verses like these as his anchors when loss and grief were raining down on him and his family:

- 1 Thessalonians 4:13—We do not mourn as ones who have no hope.

- Romans 8:31—If God is for you, who in the world can be against you?

- Philippians 1:6—He who began a good work in you will be faithful to complete it.

- Romans 8:28—God works all things for good for those who love Him and are called according to His purpose.

Do you have an anchoring verse? Or maybe an unwavering belief about God's character (such as "I know that God is faithful, no matter what"), or a hymn or worship song that the Holy Spirit often brings to mind in difficult times? If so, write it here.

What does it say to you?

RECOMMENDED READING

In preparation for Session 6, please read chapter 12 in *Fighting Your Battles* by Jonathan Evans.

FROM TEST TO TESTIMONY

Here's another excerpt from *Fighting Your Battles*, this one focusing on God's plan for your story with Him:

> Your story is one of God's tangible investments in your life. Most people meet God and want the ledger to start in the black. Most of the time, though, the ledger starts in the red and gradually moves its way to the black. So the fact that somebody you know may be in the red right now doesn't mean God isn't invested in them. By the same principle, when you see someone who has arrived at the palace, who seems like they have made it to their purpose with a great home and a great family and a great career or ministry, don't assume that you know their story. You don't know what God took them through to get them to today. Whatever He has done, I can promise you, they didn't start at the top.
>
> God's plan is to take each of us and our churches and our ministries somewhere purposeful. There are things you have gone through, things you are going through—things you must go through—to move you from the pit to the place of purpose where God wants you. The story of that journey is a testimony, and it will probably sound something like Joseph's: Somebody meant evil against you, but God meant it for good in order to bring about the present result.
>
> *Fighting Your Battles*, pages 203-204

VIDEO TEACHING NOTES

As you watch the video, use the space below to take notes. Some key points and quotes are provided as reminders.

Main Idea

- Many of the things we go through are the enemy's attempts to strip us of the evidence of our heavenly Father's favor on us. Satan wants us to feel like we've lost God's favor.

- God has a plan for your pit. He never lets those experiences go to waste. He is using your pit to prepare you, not just for the ministry to which He's called you, but for the saving of many lives.

- It's important to pay attention in the pit, because all around you is evidence of God's promise for your future—how He's going to use you. So keep your eyes open and don't give up. There are people who are going to need the comfort, the hope, and the faith that you will testify of.

- Just as God used Joseph's battle to take him to something beautiful, He will do the same for us if we remain faithful. Our hardest tests, left in God's hands, produce a testimony of God's grace, providence, goodness, and sovereignty.

- Personal Notes:

Application

No matter how bad things are, God is making it good. If it's not good yet, God's not done yet.

Quotables

- The testimony—this is where you have the ceremony because the test has been completed.

- Isn't it a blessing when you can look back over your life and see what God was doing? That the whole time, He was connecting the dots?

- When you are down to nothing, it's because God is up to something.

- Your greatest ministry is going to come out of your greatest misery. That's where your testimony comes from.

VIDEO GROUP DISCUSSION

1. "This is the fun part," says Jonathan at the beginning of this video—the testimony. This is when you finally get to see and celebrate what all the blood, sweat, and tears were for.

   What's the value of looking back over our life and seeing what God was doing, how He was connecting the dots all along? Why does this matter?

2. With Joseph's testimony in Genesis 50:20, the focus is God. The hero is God. He is the real Hero of any Christian's story. In Isaiah 46:3-4, how does the Lord describe His history with His people? What are the key verbs here that show He not only has been the Hero of their story, but has always intended to be?

   > "Listen to Me, house of Jacob, and all the remnant of the house of Israel, you who have been carried by Me from birth and have been carried from the womb; even to your old age I will be the same, and even to your graying years I will carry you! I have done it, and I will bear you; and I will carry you and I will save you."

   You can imagine the Lord saying this to you as well, because it's just as true for His people now as then. How does it make you feel to know that God Himself has been caring for you and your story throughout your life?

3. Even Jesus went through pit experiences: being betrayed, rejected, crucified; people wanting to stone Him, to throw Him off a cliff. Despite the evil, He overcame each attempt to keep Him down. In each of the verses on the next page, mark what motivated Him.

- He said this just before His crucifixion: "Now My soul has become troubled; and what am I to say? 'Father, save Me from this hour'? But for this purpose I came to this hour. Father, glorify Your name." (John 12:27-28)

- [Jesus said,] "I glorified You on the earth by accomplishing the work which You have given Me to do." (John 17:4)

- For the joy set before Him [Christ] endured the cross, despising the shame, and has sat down at the right hand of the throne of God. (Hebrews 12:2)

4. Here's a little Genesis 50 exercise of your own. In a few words or a brief sentence, list below the five most significant events or experiences of your life so far, regardless of whether they were positive or negative.

    1.

    2.

    3.

    4.

    5.

Looking back over those defining moments, which of them were pit experiences of some kind—deep, dark, and emotional?

How do you see God using the emptiness you've experienced so that nothing about your story gets wasted?

How has He helped you take those pit and palace moments to make *you* better?

Where is God continuing to refine you and sharpen you for the ministry you're doing or the ministry you envision?

How is He using your testimony to encourage someone else or to "preserve many lives"?

GROUP BIBLE EXPLORATION

1. Let's look a little more at Joseph's backstory, after he was sold into slavery by his brothers.

> Now Joseph had been taken down to Egypt; and Potiphar, an Egyptian officer of Pharaoh, the captain of the bodyguard, bought him from the Ishmaelites, who had taken him down there. And the LORD was with Joseph, so he became a successful man. And he was in the house of his master, the Egyptian. Now his master saw that the LORD was with him and that the LORD made all that he did prosper in his hand. So Joseph found favor in his sight and became his personal servant; and he made him overseer over his house, and put him in charge of all that he owned. It came about that from the time he made him overseer in his house and over all that he owned, the LORD blessed the Egyptian's house on account of Joseph; so the LORD's blessing was upon all that he owned, in the house and in the field. So he left Joseph in charge of everything that he owned; and with him there he did not concern himself with anything except the food which he ate. (Genesis 39:1-6)

> *Potiphar's wife had Joseph unjustly imprisoned, and he was thrown into another type of pit: a jail. This jail was where the king's prisoners were kept. But even there,* "the LORD was with Joseph and extended kindness to him, and gave him favor in the sight of the warden of the prison. And the warden of the prison put Joseph in charge of all the prisoners who were in the prison; so that whatever was done there, he was responsible for it. The warden of the prison did not supervise anything under Joseph's authority, because the LORD was with him; and the LORD made whatever he did prosper. (Genesis 39:21-23)

After interpreting Pharaoh's dreams when no one else in Egypt could, Pharaoh released Joseph from prison and said to his servants, "Can we find a man like this, in whom there is a divine spirit?" So Pharaoh said to Joseph, "Since God has informed you of all this, there is no one as discerning and wise as you are. You shall be in charge of my house, and all my people shall be obedient to you; only regarding the throne will I be greater than you." Pharaoh also said to Joseph, "See, I have placed you over all the land of Egypt." (Genesis 41:38-41)

What common themes do you see in Joseph's life between these three passages?

What does his example suggest about how we should conduct ourselves no matter where we've been placed?

Why is such godly consistency important for us? Why is it important out in the world?

2. Write down your biggest challenges to exercising this kind of faithfulness at work, online, or among family or friends.

Brainstorm as a group some ways to stay faithful even in the pit.

3. Like Joseph, we are stripped of many things during our lives. Paul talked about this stripping process in Philippians 3:7-10:

> Whatever things were gain to me, these things I have counted as loss because of Christ. More than that, I count all things to be loss in view of the surpassing value of knowing Christ Jesus my Lord, for whom I have suffered the loss of all things, and count them mere rubbish, so that I may gain Christ, and may be found in Him, not having a righteousness of my own derived from the Law, but that which is through faith in Christ, the righteousness which comes from God on the basis of faith, that I may know Him and the power of His resurrection and the fellowship of His sufferings.

For all that he lost, what were the greater things that he gained?

Why would he refer to his experience as partaking in the "fellowship" of Christ's sufferings?

4. We will all face pit experiences that test us and our faith in God's plan for our future. As you read through these expressions of faith from others who were in the middle of their misery, discuss what you learn from their example. Mark the specific statements that you want to cling to and carry with you as this study is coming to a close.

- I have heard the slander of many, terror is on every side; while they took counsel together against me, they schemed to take away my life. But as for me, I trust in You, LORD, I say, "You are my God." My times are in Your hand; rescue me from the hand of my enemies and from those who persecute me. Make Your face shine upon Your servant; save me in Your faithfulness. (Psalm 31:13-16)

- Beloved, do not be surprised at the fiery ordeal among you, which comes upon you for your testing, as though something strange were happening to you; but to the degree that you share the sufferings of Christ, keep on rejoicing, so that at the revelation of His glory you may also rejoice and be overjoyed. (1 Peter 4:12-14)

- Be of sober spirit, be on the alert. Your adversary, the devil, prowls around like a roaring lion, seeking someone to devour. So resist him, firm in your faith, knowing that the same experiences of suffering are being accomplished by your brothers and sisters who are in the world. After you have suffered for a little while, the God of all grace, who called you to His eternal glory in Christ, will Himself perfect, confirm, strengthen, and establish you. (1 Peter 5:8-10)

- We also celebrate in our tribulations, knowing that tribulation brings about perseverance; and perseverance, proven character; and proven character, hope; and hope does not disappoint, because the love of God has been poured out within our hearts through the Holy Spirit who was given to us. (Romans 5:3-5)

5. In your own words, what can you look forward to as you trust that God is taking you from the pit to the palace and from your misery to your ministry?

- [The redeemed of the Lord] shall give thanks to the LORD for His mercy, and for His wonders to the sons of mankind! For He has satisfied the thirsty soul, and He has filled the hungry soul with what is good. (Psalm 107:8-9)

- Light shines in the darkness for the upright; he is gracious, compassionate, and righteous…He will never be shaken;…He will not fear bad news; his heart is steadfast, trusting in the LORD. His heart is firm, he will not fear, but will look with satisfaction on his enemies. (Psalm 112:4-8)

- Blessed be the God and Father of our Lord Jesus Christ, the Father of mercies and God of all comfort, who comforts us in all our affliction so that we will be able to comfort those who are in any affliction with the comfort with which we ourselves are comforted by God. (2 Corinthians 1:3-4)

6. Jonathan offers this encouragement in his book (page 218): "God has a plan and a place for your testimony…And it will be revealed from the trials and tests, the battles and bruises, the pits and perils that you go through in this life. He's provided you with your entire story to give you a future and a hope—and someone else as well. You've been positioned and purposed to preserve somebody's life by the blood of the Lamb and the word of your testimony."

What are some ways that our testimony, our new song, helps others? Mark the answer(s) on each verse.

- [The LORD] reached down to me and heard my cry. He brought me up out of the pit of destruction, out of the mud; and He set my feet on a rock, making my footsteps firm. He put a new song in my mouth, a song of praise to our God; many will see and fear and will trust in the LORD. (Psalm 40:1-3)

- Consider Him who has endured such hostility by sinners against Himself, so that you will not grow weary and lose heart. (Hebrews 12:3)

- We will tell the generation to come the praises of the LORD, and His power and His wondrous works that He has done…so that they would put their confidence in God and not forget the works of God, but comply with His commandments, and not be like their fathers, a stubborn and rebellious generation, a generation that did not prepare its heart and whose spirit was not faithful to God. (Psalm 78:4, 7-8)

- Go up on a high mountain, Zion, messenger of good news, raise your voice forcefully, Jerusalem, messenger of good news; raise it up, do not fear. Say to the cities of Judah, "Here is your God!" (Isaiah 40:9)

- May those shout for joy and rejoice, who take delight in my vindication; and may they say continually, "The LORD be exalted, who delights in the prosperity of His servant." (Psalm 35:27)

7. Take a couple of minutes to quietly reflect on your journey with the Lord and praise Him as the psalmists did:

> God, You have taught me from my youth,
> And I still declare Your wondrous deeds…
> For Your righteousness, God, reaches to the heavens,
> You who have done great things;

God, who is like You?
(Psalm 71:17, 19)

Bless the LORD, my soul,
And all that is within me, *bless His holy name.*
Bless the LORD, my soul,
And do not forget any of His benefits;
Who pardons all your guilt,
Who heals all your diseases;
Who redeems your life from the pit,
Who crowns you with favor and compassion;
Who satisfies your years with good things.
(Psalm 103:1-5)

IN CLOSING

As you end this study, remember these six things from our sessions:

1. If God has called you, then God is for you. And if God is for you, then you can be confident that no giant can stand against you.

2. Those painful, difficult places that we've followed God to, are the places He will provide for us in. He never abandons those who are following Him. But we have to seek Him as our source and provision.

3. We can't handle the burden of battle alone. God is the owner; we are the stewards. So to fight His way means looking to heaven, relying on God to lead us to victory as we execute our assignments here on earth.

4. Jesus is in the storm with you, but you have to come to Him. He has already come and done His part—He's already walked on the chaos. Now you have to do your part. Stop thinking about your failures and your fear, and step toward the truth. Jesus is saying, "No matter what you're going through, I have one word for you: *Come.*"

5. It's time to prepare for the forecast now, not later. Because your faith *is* going to be tested. And the one whose house will still be standing rock-solid after the storm is the one who has built on God's Word and who acts on God's Word.

6. No matter how bad things are, God is making it good. If it's not good yet, God's not done yet.

Don't forget: God calls us, and He gives us everything we need to fight our giants, complete the mission, conquer the enemy, stand strong in the storm, and testify of His goodness after great injustice has been done to us. Whatever battle you're in, wherever Satan is attacking you, don't give up and don't give in, friend. Give it to God. Look to the Lord—your Champion, your Shield, your Rock, your Deliverer—and trust Him with your very life. The battle is His, and He will fight for you.

To learn more about Harvest House books and
to read sample chapters, visit our website:

www.HarvestHousePublishers.com

HARVEST HOUSE PUBLISHERS
EUGENE, OREGON